PETER SEREFINE

# So Simple Even A Politician Can Understand

## Simple ideas for seemingly complex political issues

- A Beacon Of Common Sense -
www.Liberty-Lighthouse.com

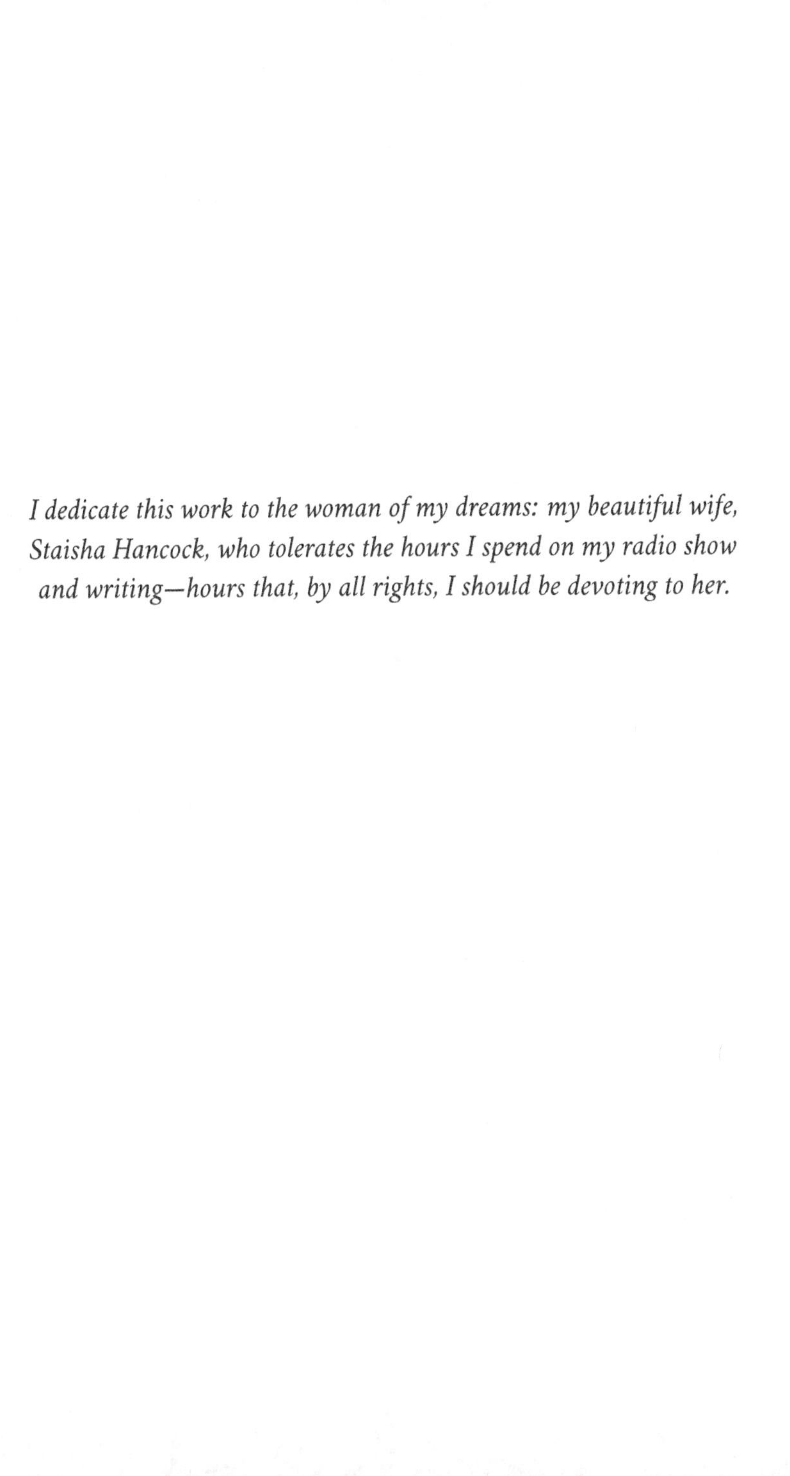

*I dedicate this work to the woman of my dreams: my beautiful wife, Staisha Hancock, who tolerates the hours I spend on my radio show and writing—hours that, by all rights, I should be devoting to her.*

# Contents


*Foreword*                                      iii
*Preface*                                        v
*Acknowledgement*                               vi


I    Fiscal Issues

  1   Unfunded Liabilities                        3
  2   Forced Philanthropy                         5
  3   Government Contracts                        7
  4   Tax on Everything                           9
  5   Fair Tax                                   11
  6   Broken Budget                              15
  7   Costly Bureaucracy                         19


II   Social Issues

  8   Minimum Wage                               25
  9   Welfare                                    28
 10   Immigration                                30
 11   Gender & Sex                               33
 12   Environmental Protection                   36

III   Unalienable Rights

13   Fake News                          41
14   Gun Control                        45
15   Voter Integrity                    49
16   One Bill, One Topic                52

Epilogue                                55
Afterword                               56
*About the Author*                      58
*Also by Peter Serefine*                59

# Foreword

This new book from Peter Serefine sports a title as self-explanatory as one can be. He even opens with the statement that "sometimes the answers we seek are so simple that we overlook them."

A series of short essays prompted by guests Mr. Serefine featured on his podcast Liberty Lighthouse, he further qualifies that he isn't presuming to have the solution, "which is why they are called ideas."

With those two introductory remarks as a guidepost, Mr. Serefine has already displayed two attributes that many of our politicians could benefit from: an eye toward clarity and a modicum of humility. However, I don't think his target audience here are members of the political class. Rather, he presents these ideas for the rest of us who find our lives affected by politicians and government.

In these pages, Mr. Serefine examines topics from money spent to legislation itself, and while the categories may be wide-ranging, they can basically be divided into the fiscal and the social. Fiscal issues such as taxation methods, government contracts, budgets, and the yoke of bureaucracy are looked at, and always with an eye toward making the confusing simple (as promised). Societal issues such as immigration and gender identity are observed as well.

Readers may disagree with some of Mr. Serefine's proposed

approaches if they so choose, but I doubt anyone can argue that perspectives like his have been too long missing from our political landscape.  Instead of playing a written game of "Mousetrap" with legislation, perhaps it's time for those responsible to assume Peter Serefine's point of view and approach.

Bill Cushing (May 24, 2021)

# Preface

Sometimes the answers we seek are so simple that we overlook them. The ideas presented in this book are just that, simple ideas that are largely overlooked. They may not be perfect solutions. They may not even be solutions at all, which is why they are called ideas. The idea for this book struck me during an interview with Cliff Oxford for my show, Liberty Lighthouse. Within a week of that interview, I had begun writing. Over the past two years of hosting Liberty Lighthouse, many simple ideas have come up. This book is a collection of those ideas.

# Acknowledgement

I would like to thank all of the guests to Liberty Lighthouse. These guests have inspired many of the ideas put forth in this book.I have had the pleasure of interviewing a presidential candidate, entrepreneurs, industry leaders, and authors in the two years I have hosted my show. These expert guests have presented ideas, inspired my own ideas, and even changed my mind on occasion. Without hosting Liberty Lighthouse, I would not have met these incredible people.

I also need to thank the owners and partners at Mojo 5-0 Radio. They were willing to take a chance on my fledgling podcast and invited me to join their group of freedom fundamentalists. Two other show hosts on Mojo 5-0 Radio, Jeremy Leahy and Mike Filip, allowed me the opportunity to fill in on their shows. Then it wasn't long until Liberty Lighthouse was broadcasting on the mighty Mojo 5-0.

# I

# Fiscal Issues

*On October 17th, 2020, when Don Blankenship, 2020 presidential candidate for the Constitution Party, was on Liberty Lighthouse he was asked how he would tackle the national debt. His answer was, "Just like you eat an elephant, one bite at a time." In part I, we will look at some ideas for what some of those bites could look like.*

# 1

# Unfunded Liabilities

USDebtClock.org reports the national debt is $28 trillion, and the republic has another $147 trillion in unfunded liabilities (a trillion has twelve zeros, in case you were wondering). Our debt is 128% of the nation's gross domestic product. If you are a taxpayer, your portion of the debt is approaching $250,000 and the unfunded liabilities are an additional $450,000 per citizen. By the time this book has made its way into your hands, I am sure all of those numbers have gone way up. No nation in the history of the world has ever survived a debt-to-income ratio even close to that unbalanced. Washington DC continues to spend money faster than they can print it. This absolutely must stop for We The People to have a chance of remaining free people.

Every year our federal government budgets a deficit. They actually plan on spending more money than they will bring in. In addition, we pay over $300 billion a year in interest on the national debt. That is the fastest-growing line in the federal budget, yet we continue to run a deficit.

Politicians have completely given up on fiscal responsibility.

Our elected officials frequently put forth legislation with no proposed method of payment. Free college, free healthcare, and guaranteed minimum income are just a few of the ideas put forth that we don't have the money for.

One simple idea that came about from a conversation with prize-winning poet, Bill Cushing[1], is to require lawmakers to explain how a bill would be paid for. Any bill proposed that spends any money would have to explain where that money was coming from or how it would be raised. Bill's idea doesn't require a constitutional amendment or ever a law to pass Congress. This could be accomplished by making a rule in the House of Representatives.

* * *

---

[1] Bill Cushing has been a guest on Liberty Lighthouse three times. His most recent appearance was May 1st, 2021.

# 2

# Forced Philanthropy

With the budget deficit, national debt, and unfunded liability issues discussed in the last chapter, where do we cut? What is the first bite of that enormous elephant? When asked these questions most people immediately attack the three largest line items in the budget: Medicare & Medicaid, Social Security, and National Defense. Any proposal to cut any of those three is political suicide.

It seems politicians have decided that any spending cut anywhere in the budget that does not attack the three biggest line items just isn't worth doing. That is ridiculous. Saving a dollar on pens is the same as saving a dollar on fighter jets.

The idea to help in this area is going to sound harsh. Stop giving federal money to non-profit organizations. According to the National Council of Nonprofits, 80% of the money going into non-profits comes from the government.

Giving taxpayer money to a non-profit is forcing taxpayers to "donate." If the non-profit is a worthy cause, then it should be capable of raising money itself. Think about the political implications of tax money funding non-profits. Every taxpayer should not be forced to fund Planned Parenthood, the National Rifle Association, museums, lobby groups, and professional sports, just to name a few.

Politics makes the idea of forced philanthropy even more disturbing. Many of these organizations get our tax money and they are politically active. They take your tax dollars and then donate to political causes and campaigns. Your tax dollars may very well be financing political issues or even political candidates that you do not agree with.

* * *

3

# Government Contracts

Let's examine another area where a small bite of the debt elephant might be possible. Federal law requires fair and open competition for the majority of procurement. That makes sense. Without such law, nepotism, favoritism, and paying back favors would be rampant. Without the requirement of competition, governments could easily waste money on everything it buys, but does government follow its own law?

The portion of spending by the Department of Defense that goes through the open bidding process has declined every year since 2008. By 2016, more than half of the DoD's spending did not go through an open procurement process. In 2017, the Veteran's Affairs office awarded a $1 billion contract for electronic health records keeping without considering any other sources. The Federal Emergency Management Agency awarded $46 million for response to hurricane Katrina without considering an alternative.

The federal government is not the only offender avoiding competition. A quick internet search will reveal many examples of state and local governments awarding contracts without allowing competition. The state of California awarded $282 million to private contractors last year alone. The coronavirus pandemic spurred no-bid contract awards all over the country. From your local school board all the way up through federal departments, governments seem to pick and choose when to allow the required competition.

Our governments spend our money without competition because of vague exceptions in the law. Vague exceptions are exploited by corrupt politicians. One exception is if there is no other source. You cannot possibly know that there is not another source if you don't look. Applied Energetics was awarded a contract for a system to detonate roadside bombs. The Tucson-based company won a $50 million contract to shoot lightning at improvised explosive devices. The company got the contract under the claim of no other source exception. A competitor, Indiana-based Xtreme Alternative Defense Systems developed a similar system that was significantly cheaper. That second company would have saved some of our tax dollars.

The idea in this chapter is not new at all. In fact, the idea here is simply to follow the existing law. Require all government spending at all levels to go through an open bidding process. Clearly define any exceptions in specific terms and require an exception to go through a strict approval process.

* * *

# 4

# Tax on Everything

How much of your income goes to income tax is easy to figure out. Adding up taxes that are paid as sales tax or the tax on a utility bill is a little more work, but can still be accomplished. However, trying to calculate how much of your money goes to paying some federal tax or fee that is not clearly identified is nearly impossible.

For example, trying to calculate how much your grocery bill is inflated because of the corporate income tax on the manufacturer, distributors, warehouses, and stores is daunting. Then add the fuel tax passed along through the distribution costs.

Regulatory fees, property tax, and license costs are other forms of tax included in the cost of doing business, and they're included in the cost of everything you buy. After all, an inconvenient truth is that We The People pay all taxes one way or another.

Import tariffs, vehicle registrations, gasoline tax, vice taxes like those on alcohol and cigarettes all add up. Travel taxes and hotel tax are added to your vacation costs. It doesn't matter if you rent or own, you either pay property tax directly or property tax is added into the cost of your rent.

Income tax, social security tax, medicare tax, and unemployment tax are all collected and paid before seeing your paycheck. Then more taxes and fees are included in every purchase you make. Even after you die, you're still paying tax. Your funeral service and your coffin will both be taxed. If you've been fortunate enough to save a few dollars you'll pay inheritance tax too.

Remember the Boston Tea Party? The rebellious act that preceded the American Revolution was to protest the Tea Act of 1773. That was over a tax on what was essentially one luxury item. The Tea Act levied a six pence tax per pound of tea imported to the British Colonies. That would be about $2.50 per pound today. In total, the Tea Act would have cost the thirteenth colonies less than $300,000 a year in today's dollars. Imagine how those rebels would feel in today's United States where absolutely everything is taxed and retaxed.

Government should be restricted to one simple form of tax. Pick one, any one: consumption tax, income tax, import tariffs, or whatever. A single form of tax would allow taxpayers to know how much we really pay. Federal, state, county, and local governments all using a single form of tax.

The next chapter will discuss one proposal of what a single federal consumption-based tax could look like.

* * *

5

# Fair Tax

Everyone would agree that the government needs money. How the government gets that money has been argued since the beginning of time. Taxing income forcibly funds the government before the citizens even see the money. Many consider income tax to be unjust. Many more people consider the graduated rates of income even more unjust. Increased tax rates on successful people punishes success itself. For that reason, some prefer a flat tax, which would still be an income tax, just a flat rate regardless of income. Let's look at a brief history of income tax in the United States.

Federal income tax was overturned by the US Supreme Court as unconstitutional in 1894. In 1913, the sixteenth amendment to the Constitution made direct federal income tax legal. By the end of that year, federal income tax was passed into law and instituted.At the time, President Woodrow Wilson said the basic income tax would never rise above one percent. He was obviously very wrong.

The income tax imposed in 1913 was only one percent on income above $3,000 per year. Adjusting for inflation, $3,000 in 1913 has the buying power of over $80,000 in 2021. Less than three percent of citizens earned enough to pay the first income tax. By contrast, today anyone earning over $12,000 a year is required to file a tax return and according to Tax Policy Center, 56% of people pay income tax.

There were six increasing tax brackets in the 1913 income tax. Each bracket required an additional one percent tax. The increases happened at $20,000, $50,000, $75,000, $100,000, $250,000, and $500,000 or more. Adjusting for inflation, if you earned over $13 million per year you would be in the highest tax bracket of six percent.

The Communist Manifesto, originally the Manifesto of the Communist Party, is an 1848 pamphlet by German philosophers Karl Marx and Friedrich Engels. This pamphlet spelled out the steps to a communist takeover. Step two in that list is "a heavy progressive or graduated income tax." Just 65 years after the Communist Manifesto was published, the United States instituted a graduated, or progressive, income tax. In fact, many of the arguments used by the supporters of the income tax mirrored Marx. Make the rich pay their fair share and soak the rich were arguments used then and being heard again now.

To make income tax even more controversial, the current tax code is about 44,000 pages long. To put that into perspective, the average bible is around 1,200 pages. So the US tax code is longer than thirty-six copies of the bible. It is so long and so complex that only the wealthy can afford specialized attorneys to decipher it.

You might ask, why is the US Tax Code so long? Partly because of loopholes and favors for special interest groups. Partly because, as stated earlier, the government does not do "simple" anymore. Partly to attempt to control We The People.

Tax credits, tax rebates, and tax deductions are all used to influence your behavior and reward specific favored industries.

Between the unfairness of the tax code itself, the punishment of success by the graduated rates, and the feeling of theft before even receiving your paycheck, there is no wonder the IRS is probably the most hated agency in the United States.

Adam Yomtov[2], New York State Volunteer Director of the National Retail Sales Tax Alliance, came to the Liberty Lighthouse to discuss an alternative. The idea is called Fair Tax. It is a one-time tax on new goods and services only. First introduced in Congress in 1999, the Fair Tax would replace the federal income tax, Social Security tax, Medicare tax, corporate tax, gift tax, capital gains tax, estate tax, and alternative minimum tax. This very concept would give consumers a modicum of control over how much tax they pay. You can choose to pay tax on a new $300,000 car, or pay tax on a new $30,000 car, or avoid paying the tax at all by buying a used car.

The first objection to a consumption tax is that it unfairly hurts the poor. HR 25, the Fair Tax bill, addresses that plan rather ingeniously. Everyone gets a monthly tax rebate based on the poverty level. No loopholes. No deductions. No favors.No graduated punishment. No manipulation. The income tax goes away, and with it, the IRS as we know it. In fact, HR 25 even disappears if the government is unwilling or unable to repeal the 16th amendment, thereby removing the possibility of ever having both a consumption tax and an income tax.

A flat-rate income tax would be an improvement over the current system, but the Fair Tax builds a whole new and more

---

[2]  Adam Yomtov was heard on Liberty Lighthouse on May 1st, 2020

just system.

* * *

# 6

# Broken Budget

In the 244 years since the foundation of our republic, we have been a debt-free nation a total of once—and only for two years. President Andrew Jackson was the only president in our history able to claim that victory, in 1835 and 1836. The United States has had the world's largest economy since 1871 but we clearly can't manage it.

The Congressional Budget Office reports the United States federal budget now tops $4 trillion annually.That means our federal government spends $11 billion per day. To put that into perspective, if you spend $1 million a day, every day, it would take you just shy of 11,000 years to spend $4 trillion. If you spend $1 billion a day, it would still take 4,000 years to spend $4 trillion, and our federal government spends that every year. None of that even considers the trillions of dollars spent on coronavirus response or the multiple proposals by the current administration to spend trillions more.

With this insurmountable debt, our federal government continues to run a deficit. Congress votes to raise its own debt ceiling constantly.Our elected officials make absolutely no effort to run a balanced budget. A Townhall poll from March 2013 says that 85% of citizens supported the idea of a balanced budget amendment to the constitution, but Congress hasn't even taken that idea seriously. Here is a simple example of what that could look like. This example is from the simulated Convention of States hosted by COS Action.

> SECTION 1. The public debt shall not be increased except upon a recorded vote of two-thirds of each house of Congress and only for a period not to exceed one year.
>
> SECTION 2. No state or any subdivision thereof shall be compelled or coerced by Congress or the President to appropriate money.

Since that idea seems like a dream, let's just move along. How about just a budget? Congress doesn't even do that anymore. What they call a budget is just a bunch of spending bills. Spending alone does not a budget make. A budget is a comparison of both income and expenses. The last time our federal government passed an actual budget was 2006. The last time there was a balanced budget, meaning a budget that didn't start out planning on a deficit, was 2001. That was twenty years ago. Imagine if you ran your personal finances like that. Imagine if you spent more money than you made every year for 20 consecutive years.

The budget process in Washington DC is clearly broken. Not only can the 12 congressional subcommittees not restrain the spending below the tax revenue line, but they can't do it on time either. Since 1997, the federal government has not been able to pass more than one-third of the budget on time. The deadline does not change. All portions of the budget are to be passed before the beginning of the new fiscal year on October first every year. If the federal government were half of a marriage, the spouse would have left a long time ago over this kind of financial mismanagement.

So, Washington can't pass a complete budget, can't pass spending bills on time, can't stay within a budget. Spending is completely out of control, and Congress doesn't even question the process. Most of last year's line-item spending will most likely be next year's spending plus some percentage. Twelve different subcommittees and all of the results are the same, year after year. Spend too much and never hold any office accountable. Between congressional salaries, staff salaries, and office administration costs, Congress itself costs the taxpayers $2 million a day, every day. For $2 million a day, members should be able to pass a budget on time. For $2 million a day, they should be able to come up with a plan to shrink the national debt.

During a conversation with entrepreneur and author Cliff Oxford[3], a simple idea came up. An idea used in business. Some businesses do this every year; some do it once every few years; some only do it if they have financial trouble. It is called a zero-sum budget. It is a very simple concept. Every agency, office, and department starts out with $0 in the budget. The office has to justify every dollar that they will be awarded in the next year's budget. Instead of just automatically getting last year's amount plus some percent increase, the office has to explain how much money it needs and how it will spend that money.

---

[3]  Cliff Oxford appeared on Liberty Lighthouse on May 8th, 2021

Using a zero-sum budget process won't stop government overspending, but at least it would force someone in government to look at and justify spending.

* * *

7

## Costly Bureaucracy

Bureaucracy is expensive and wasteful. Every layer of middle management and paper pushers is another layer of payroll. The cost of bureaucracy in the healthcare system came up in a conversation with Ed Eichhorn[4]. That same cost of bureaucracy is reminiscent of the ridiculous and countless layers built into our ever-growing government.

Federal redundancy is a simple place to start. There are several federal government offices that have nearly identical missions. This is an obvious waste of time and money. Then there is the redundancy between layers of government. There is the Federal Environmental Protection Agency, yet every state also has a state-level version of the EPA. Cutting back on redundant workloads is low hanging fruit of the wasteful bureaucracy tree.

Next, we are going to discuss just one system that not only wastes money on unnecessary layers but also mimics a

---

[4]  Ed Eichhorn, the coauthor of "Healing American Healthcare", appeared on Liberty Lighthouse on May 15th, 2021.

19

communistic system in the level of control and manipulation it affords.

Most taxpayers pay income tax to our federal, state, and local governments. Some of us also pay at the county level. Some of us are fortunate enough to live in jurisdictions that don't tax income: the point being, income tax is already paid at many different levels. So then, why are most state and local government budgets funded by federal money? On average, state, county, and local government budgets are 30% funded by federal tax dollars.

Let's look at the flow of that money. First, taxpayers pay the Internal Revenue Service. The IRS employs the equivalent of 73,000 full-time employees. These employees collect the money and turn it over to Congress. Congress divides that money between the approximately 440 federal departments and agencies. State and local governments write grant requests to many of those federal offices. Requests are reviewed at the federal level, and if approved, your tax money is then awarded back down to your town where the journey began. Every step in the process just outlined costs money. There are employees and office expenses at every point in that circular process. What a costly waste.

The federal government collects your tax money and then uses it to manipulate the behavior of state and local governments. President Reagan famously threatened to withhold federal highway money from states unless states raised the legal drinking age to 21. President Obama threatened to withhold education money over transgender issues. The EPA, DOT, OSHA, and other agencies award grants to get a desired result. The flow of money is socialistic in nature, but the manipulation and control that the flow of money affords are almost communistic.

This circular flow of tax money needs to stop. The first thing it does best is waste a significant portion of our money paying for the levels of bureaucracy. Secondly, the current system gives the federal government too much power. State, county, and local governments need to become self-sufficient. They should collect their own taxes and fund their own projects. Reduce the federal income tax by the amount doled back to state and local governments. Then allow those jurisdictions to fund their own governments. Keep the tax revenue in the government closest to the people and end the manipulation, control, and wasteful bureaucracy of the federal government.

* * *

# II

# Social Issues

*Many people believe that political issues are downstream of social issues. The theory is that politics respond to the culture and not the other way around. In part II, we will discuss political ideas to deal with social issues.*

8

# Minimum Wage

The federal minimum wage is a shining example of federalism. Federal law sets the minimum of minimums while each state, county, and municipality has the power and the right to raise its own minimum wage above the federal minimum. This is how our federalist system of government is supposed to work. The cost of living varies wildly from state to state and from city to town, so there is no reason to think that a single minimum wage would suffice in every locality in our vast republic.

Lately, there is a big push to raise the federal minimum wage to $15 per hour and make it a living wage. Proponents of this idea argue that you can't raise a family at the current $7.25 per hour. One talking point often says that nobody working forty hours a week should live below the poverty line. Let's begin with some history.

The first federal minimum wage in the United States was set by Franklin Delano Roosevelt in 1933, as part of the new deal, but was declared unconstitutional. The idea was reworked and became law again in 1938 at $0.25 per hour. In 1938, that was the equivalent buying power of just short of $5 today. That is definitely not enough to raise a family on and was not supposed to be.

The current $7.25 per hour minimum wage was set in 2009. That was 12 years ago. It is probably time to consider an adjustment because $7.25 in 2009 has the equivalent buying power of $8.64 today. That is a far cry from the $15 per hour being proposed as a living wage.

In the United States, the poverty level is set by the federal Department of Health and Human Services. The current poverty threshold for a single person is $12,060 per year. Divide that into a standard forty-hour workweek and you come up with $5.80 per hour. So the current federal minimum wage clearly exceeds the federal poverty threshold. Most would logically argue that is the exact purpose of the federal minimum wage. Therefore, the argument that nobody should work full-time and live below the poverty line is a straw man argument.

What about that "raise a family" argument? That is not the purpose of the minimum wage. The federal minimum wage is the minimum of minimums. It is not made for raising a family and should not be. If the minimum wage was set to keep a family of four out of poverty then those without families and those with smaller families would disproportionately benefit. Where do you draw that line? Why set a living wage based on a family of four when there are clearly families of more than four?

The federalist concept behind the minimum wage is the beauty of it. It clearly costs far more to live in Washington DC or New York City than it does to live in Jackson, Minnesota or Bellefonte, Pennsylvania. That is why many states and municipalities have set a minimum wage above the federal level. The federal minimum wage is irrelevant in any jurisdiction that has raised its own minimum wage.

The simple idea being presented not only sets the federal minimum wage at a reasonable level but also removes future debate about setting the federal minimum wage. Tie the federal minimum wage to the poverty line and legislate that it adjusts automatically with the federal poverty line. Congress can pass one minimum wage law and never deal with it again.

If we assume the current $7.25 federal minimum wage was appropriate when it was set in 2009 and adjust for inflation, the resulting $8.64 is about 150% of the poverty threshold for a single person set by the Department of Health and Human Services in 2020. So, Congress should pass a law setting the minimum wage to 150% of the poverty line for a single person and set the minimum wage to automatically adjust at the beginning of each fiscal year. On October 1, every year, the minimum wage automatically adjusts based on the most recent report from the Department of Health and Human Services; thus this fight is resolved forever, and there is one less thing for Congress to use as a bargaining chip.

$$* * *$$

# 9

# Welfare

Disability and welfare are often conflated. For the purpose of this conversation, welfare refers only to the assistance afforded to able-bodied people capable of working. Those who are disabled and incapable of working should be cared for.

The world is a cruel place. Sometimes people need help. Government should absolutely be there when help is needed, temporarily. Therein lies the first point of this chapter. Welfare should be temporary. Any and all government subsidies should be temporary with a focused goal of making the individual self-sufficient again.

Many people believe that we are becoming a welfare state. History has shown that a welfare state cannot long survive. President Lyndon Johnson started the war on poverty in 1964. Our federal government now spends about $1 trillion dollars a year, spread across about 100 different programs, in the name of fighting poverty. In fact, since its inception, the war on poverty has cost taxpayers an estimated $23 trillion. The result of this war is no discernable difference in the poverty level.

Living on public assistance has become generational for some families. The system certainly isn't working to end poverty by helping people become self-sufficient. Prominent black conservatives even blame the welfare system for a significant portion of the erosion of black families and black communities. Continued generational usage of public aid would suggest that maybe it is too comfortable. Supplemental food assistance, housing assistance, help with utilities, cash payments, medical assistance, and who knows what else those 100 different programs may offer. Given the dysfunction in our bloated overly bureaucratic government system, the likelihood that these 100 different offices communicate is almost zero.

Using the same concept discussed in the chapter on minimum wage, tie welfare to the Department of Health and Human Services poverty line. The sum total of all welfare, assistance and aid should be considered together. The total amount should be limited to, say, 150% of the poverty threshold upon approval. Then, on a set pre-defined schedule, the total should follow a systematic reduction in benefits over time, all while offering occupational assistance, career placement, and educational help. Helping welfare recipients become self-sufficient not only helps the recipient but also helps their family, the community, the economy, and society as a whole.

* * *

# 10

# Immigration

Immigration is an issue that the federal government does not want to solve. Politicians actually want the fight. Even during the migrant surge of the early 1900s immigrants had to meet basic standards before they were allowed into the United States. At different times in our national history, we have screened immigrants for diseases and parasites and even required that immigrants had a certain amount of money when they arrived. Today one side wants to let anyone who shows up in while the other side demands immigrants follow prescribed procedures.

Democrats who once favored a southern border wall now say one would be racists. Presidents pick and choose to what extent they will enforce immigration laws while Congress refuses to pass laws of any significance. Meanwhile, progressive politicians continuously attempt to change the very langue around the controversy.

Political correctness mandates illegal aliens be referred to as undocumented immigrants. Rather than change the laws so that legal immigration is easier, progressives change the language so we forget that any laws are broken. Criminals with a final deportation order against them don't have their work permits revoked. Those in the United States illegally are allowed to find employment and in some states are provided benefits like taxpayer-funded healthcare.

The current administration sent a message that the borders were open to all. The resulting influx of migrants was overwhelming to the very Immigration and Customs Enforcement agencies that the left has lobbied to abolish.Rather than a crackdown on the border itself, the Vice President is attempting to work with Central American governments to fix the "core of the problem" and make the home countries better.Somehow, the administration thinks offering more money to foreign countries will make the United States less appealing to potential migrants.

The United States has always welcomed hard-working immigrants with dreams of a better life.The people fleeing their homes are not to blame. To much of the impoverished of the world, the United States is the shining city on the hill.

A simple idea that has been presented many times would have a huge impact on illegal immigration.In 1996 the E-Verify system was launched. E-Verify allows employers to complete the required I-9 form online when hiring new employees. The system verifies your potential new employee is legally eligible to work in the United States. Employers who use the E-Verify system are afforded protection from accidentally hiring someone not authorized to work in the United States.

The I-9 form is required during hiring but the use of the E-Verify system is not. Politicians have argued about making the use of E-Verify mandatory for at least a decade, but as stated earlier, politicians want the immigration fight. If illegal aliens were not able to find work, there would be a powerful incentive to immigrate legally. Though not a solution to illegal immigration, widespread use of the E-Verify system would be a powerful deterrent and would not cost the taxpayers anything. The system already exists.

Mandate the use of the E-Verify system during the hiring process.

* * *

# 11

# Gender & Sex

Sex and gender were synonymous for all of human existence until the end of the twentieth century. Now progressives have redefined gender into a social construct.

Regardless of your opinion of the new definition, the fact remains that males and females are different. Male and female sports were set up because of these differences. No matter how many drugs or hormones a person takes, the playing field is not leveled.A biological boy competing in a girl's sport will have a physical advantage. Allowing a biological boy to compete against girls is not fair to the girls and should outrage feminists.

Transgender females have been allowed to compete with biological girls. Those transgendered women have dominated their sport. They have easily broken records previously held by women. Transgender athletes are winning competitions and titles. In Connecticut, for example, two transgendered high school girls have broken fifteen records previously held by nine different girls. Biological girls are being hurt emotionally by the unfair competition and financially by missing out on scholarship opportunities. In some sports, like Mixed Martial

Arts, women are being physically hurt too. Trans-gender Fallon Fox literally broke the skull of her opponent in a brutal match that was stopped by the official in just two minutes.

The military is another area where we need to be concerned. A recent report showed that 44% of women failed the new gender-neutral combat readiness physical test for the US Army while only 7% of men failed. The readiness of the military cannot be weakened in the name of equity and inclusion. If a woman wishes to become a Navy SEAL, for example, she should be held to the same standards as the men. Anything less is dangerous for the team and for national security. National defense is no place for socially engineered studies of equity.

There are two ways to handle this situation. The first idea is that we embrace the new definition. If society embraces the idea that gender is a social construct of the roles we play, then don't use that definition to classify sports. Simply use biological sex as the separator. Divide sports by those who have ever had a penis and those who have not. Athletes can identify as whatever gender they choose but must compete by biological sex. Don't ask for gender on job applications or any other forms. Ask for biological sex. This seems to be the method many states are adopting. Male and female sports can still exist, and feminism survives.

The second way to handle the new definition is to make it irrelevant. Eliminate all division by sex or gender. Want to be a Marine? Fine, here are the requirements regardless of sex or gender identity. Want to play professional basketball? Okay. Everyone competes for a spot in the NBA. This idea is not fair to women, but progress is destroying feminism anyway. Fewer women will qualify for sports or pass basic military training, but double standards will no longer be a problem.

Either idea ends the fabricated debate. After all, if gender is a social construct, then society can choose when or if gender should be considered.

* * *

# 12

# Environmental Protection

Everyone agrees that we need clean air and clean water to survive. No one of any political stripe can argue otherwise. The disagreement occurs over how to achieve the goal of clean air and clean water. Terms like global cooling, global warming, or climate change fuel the argument of the role of government in reaching the stated goal.

The government's bureaucracy is again a problem. Many departments, agencies, and offices attempt to regulate behavior to save the planet. It is no longer just the federal Environmental Protection Agency working toward the goal, but also state EPAs. Presidents get involved by executive actions. Other offices and officials write regulations and Congress passes laws. With many sources of rules, it is impossible to keep up.

Take automotive manufacturing as an example that we can all relate to. The Environmental Protection Agency sets one set of standards and rules. The National Highway Traffic Safety Administration sets other standards. Then the President comes along and signs an executive order to set a different standard.

For example, the President may say that new passenger cars

have to get thirty miles per gallon by next year and the EPA says that CO2 emissions must be below 300 grams per mile traveled. Those two rules are fine by themselves, but that is not where our government stops.

Another rule requires that your passenger car has a catalytic converter. While a catalytic converter helps control emissions, it robs the vehicle of power. Many required pieces of pollution control equipment adversely affect a vehicle's power and fuel economy while reducing emissions. Reducing power means the engine must burn more gas to go the same distance. If the required pollution control devices reduce emissions by 50% but also reduces power by 50%, the net result is zero change to emissions.

In the mid-1970s, small Japanese import cars were getting over thirty miles to the gallon of gasoline.That was before most of the environmental protection laws were enacted. Given the advancements of technology since the mid-1970s, imagine how far a small car could go on a gallon of gas today if left unrestricted.Just the expended use of aluminum, plastics, and carbon fiber materials has made cars significantly lighter over the past forty years. Fuel injection and computer-controlled ignition timing are two other technological advances that increased fuel economy. If a comparable vehicle were manufactured today and could get sixty miles per gallon, that would be double the fuel economy and would therefore produce half of the emissions.

So many people in so many offices need to virtue signal that they are part of the solution. They all need to make the next rule to protect our air from the filthy internal combustion engine. Simple ideas have escaped all of these people. The goal is clean air, not more rules.

The simple version of emissions control is set in a single goal line. For example, new passenger cars sold in the United States cannot emit more than 250 grams of carbon per mile traveled. Let the expert mechanics, engineers, and designers that make the cars figure out how to get below the line. Allow the industry experts to increase fuel economy and limit emissions through innovation. In short, get the government out of the way and allow the ingenuity of the American worker to be unleashed to actually solve problems. Allowed the opportunity, the free market can accomplish more than any government program or law.

****

# III

# Unalienable Rights

*According to the Declaration of Independence, governments are instituted among men to secure our unalienable rights. Part III is ideas to accomplish just that.*

# 13

# Fake News

Fake and biased news has existed since the beginning of time. Ancient empires exaggerated their conquests and downplayed their failures. Traveling minstrels sang stories of glory that became more embellished as they traveled. Many US Presidents have struggled with misleading news stories. The 1800 presidential race between Jefferson and Adams was filled with exaggerations and lies. Abraham Lincoln struggled with fake news pamphlets circulated to destroy his administration. President Trump pointed out what he considered to be fake news and fake news outlets zealously.

What the problem really boils down to is human nature extended across time. All people have an inherent bias. Reporters and journalists are charged with the difficult task of setting aside their own personal biases. With the instant gratification afforded by modern social media and decades of complacency in the United States political scene, unbiased reporting is nearly dead. It has become increasingly easy to see the bias in news programming. Stories are ignored because the show host or the network just doesn't like the story. Details are exaggerated.

Big bold claims are made in headlines for stories that do not even come close to supporting that headline.

Modern news outlets don't just twist individual stories. The manipulation of what is published now involves coordinated narratives.No matter which side of the political aisle an outlet supports, nearly everything published is massaged and twisted to support the organization's political views. Not only are the editorials and commentaries forced into these greater narrative molds, but stories and programs that claim to be news are as well.

All of this manipulation helps to further divide We The People. It can be extremely time-consuming to research a news story from multiple outlets of multiple sides, trying to decode the articles and filter out facts from opinions. Modern social media exacerbates this challenge. Anyone with internet access can post what they believe to be news. Far too many people get the majority of their news from social media. The recent advent of so-called fact-checkers has not helped. Over and over again the organizations providing the fact checks have been proven to push a political narrative.

Journalists, reporters, and news anchors have the same constitutionally protected right of free speech that the rest of us have. Free speech protects your right to manipulate and lie if that is what you choose to do. Misinformation, disinformation, and hate speech are all unalienable rights. The right to free speech is integral to the freedom of the United States. That creates a challenge where consuming news is concerned.

The one slightly fuzzy area is considering the company and owners of the company. We temporarily waive our right to free speech from time to time. Your boss, for example, can restrict your speech while you are at work. While at work, you represent the company and therefore they set rules to protect the company. News media companies could be held liable for intentional or flagrant misinformation in their reporting.

There was a time in our nation when unbiased reporting was law. From 1949 until 1987 anyone with a broadcast license was required to show both sides of controversial issues under the Fairness Doctrine. This Federal Communications Commission rule could be very challenging at times. What was or was not considered a controversial issue could change. A broadcaster might say something that he or she did not think was controversial only to find out that the station manager received several phone calls about the statement. Complaints and threats of complaints to the FCC became burdensome. Opinion shows nearly went extinct during the years of the Fairness Doctrine. Entire radio stations and networks just switched to music-only formats, sometimes overnight.

In 1987, President Ronald Reagan suspended the Fairness Doctrine. The reason Reagan gave publicly for his decision was that the rules unfairly restricted the freedom of speech. Some speculate whether Reagan's stated motives were genuine. For our purposes, his motives are irrelevant. The important part is that, with the fairness doctrine suspended, opinion broadcasting became possible again. Radio talk shows came back on the airways, and news shows started inserting opinions again.

Kim "Kid" Curry[5] was a top 40 disc jockey for many years in some pretty impressive markets. He recently wrote a book called "The Death of Fairness" where he advocates for the return of the Fairness Doctrine. Those on the right side of the political

---

[5]  Kim "Kid" Curry was heard on Liberty Lighthouse on March 27th, 2020.

aisle are sternly against this idea. The Fairness Doctrine as it existed would kill conservative talk radio and much of the programming on television news networks. Kim Curry makes some very good points though. There is no place to go for fair unbiased reporting in today's United States. If the Fairness Doctrine was revived only for the broadcast airways, we may have that place again.

The key part of Mr. Curry's idea that makes it tolerable to some conservatives is the restriction on the scope of a new Fairness Doctrine. If the rules could come back and only apply to FCC license holders, they would not apply to satellite, cable, and internet broadcasts. Local television and radio stations would be the only outlets covered by these rules. Therefore, your local television and radio stations would become a place where we could see both sides of an issue without needing to search out sources of opposing views.

Opinion shows could still exist, just not broadcast over the airways. If the FCC would give up trying to regulate cable, satellite, and internet communications, this might work. Conservatives are predictably skeptical about that "if." Government agencies are prone to expanding their power and reach. The fear is that if a new Fairness Doctrine were implemented, it would eventually be expanded to cable, satellite, and internet providers is a completely reasonable fear.

* * *

# 14

# Gun Control

The first successful semi-automatic rifle was released in 1885 by an Austrian-born gunsmith. In 1907, Winchester released a semi-automatic rifle with removable magazines and continued to produce the Winchester model 1907 until 1957. The year 1911 saw the United States military adopt the semi-automatic pistol as the standard sidearm that would be used for the next seventy-five years. The 1911 design by Colt is still incredibly popular today. In 1917 a semi-automatic rifle became widely used by French military forces. Today, semi-automatic weapons are commonplace.

For 143 years, the Second Amendment was the only federal firearms law. In 1934, President Franklin Delano Roosevelt changed that. The National Firearms Act was flawed and needed to be modified repeatedly. The end result was a $200 tax and FBI background check to own short-barreled rifles and shotguns, fully automatic firearms, mufflers, and silencers. Contrary to popular belief, all of these things are still legal. They just require an additional background check and a $200 tax stamp.

Just 34 years after the Federal Firearms Act, the federal government tried again. In 1968, following the assassination of President Kennedy, President Lyndon Johnson signed the Gun Control Act of 1968. This law added destructive devices like bombs and grenades to the list of weapons requiring an FBI background check and a $200 tax. The Gun Control Act of 1968 also set the age requirement for handguns to 21, mandated serial numbers, and began the list of what are now know as prohibited possessors.It also banned the importation of firearms with "no sporting purpose." It's interesting to note that before 1968 anyone could buy a firearm through a catalog and have it delivered by the US Postal Service right to the door.

Eighteen years later, in 1986, the Firearm Owners Protection Act was passed by Congress.This law further defines machine guns and silencers, yet again. It also expressly prohibits a national database of dealer records or a database of firearms.

Only seven years pass before the Brady Bill—officially the Brady Handgun Violence Prevention Act was signed by President Clinton—this law further amends the Gun Control Act and requires that background checks be completed before a gun is purchased from a licensed dealer. It established the National Instant Criminal Background Check System (NICS), which is maintained by the FBI and used by federally licensed firearms dealers and by many sheriff departments when issuing concealed carry permits.

Only one year later, in 1994, President Clinton signed the Public Safety and Recreational Firearms Use Protection Act. More commonly known as the "Assault Weapons Ban," this law expired in 2004. Many attempts have been made to renew this law. The current president has called for the renewal of the law repeatedly.

The years 2003 and 2005 saw laws that dealt with dealers and manufacturers but not citizens. Then in 2008, the Supreme Court heard District of Columbia v. Heller and overturned a handgun ban in Washington DC.

Gun control advocates have pushed for banning certain types of firearms seemingly forever. Right now the push is to ban semi-automatic assault rifles. In the 1980s, the movement began going after handguns. Proposals have been made to tax firearms annually and limit both firearm and ammunition purchases. Supporters of the Second Amendment claim that banning any weapon is a violation of the right to keep and bear arms. Let's be honest. Nobody wants the emotionally troubled teenager next door to build a nuclear weapon in the basement. So, the debate is really about where to draw the line.

Dr. Val Finnell [6] is the Pennsylvania Director of Gun Owners of America. He was a guest on Liberty Lighthouse. During that conversation, a simple idea arose, one that both clearly draws the line in question and addresses concerns about the militarization of police. Any firearm, weapon, or equipment available to state and local law enforcement agencies must be made available for private sale without additional tax or bureaucratic requirements.

The right to keep and bear arms protected by the Second Amendment exists solely for the purpose of standing up to tyranny. In the event we need to defend ourselves from a tyrannical government, it will most likely be the state and local law enforcement called upon to confiscate guns. So, it is state and local law enforcement agencies we will need to defend against first. We The People must be allowed to be equally

---

[6]  Dr. Val Finnell appeared on the Liberty Lighthouse on April 24th, 2021

equipped.

So, if private citizens can't own semi-automatic rifles, grenade launchers, or armored vehicles, neither can law enforcement. Limiting magazine capacity for citizens will limit magazine capacity for police. Tasers, stun guns, body armor, mace, etc. whatever law enforcement can buy, citizens can buy and for the same price without extra requirements.

* * *

# 15

# Voter Integrity

The right to vote is sacred and fundamental to our system of government. Voter fraud has been a recurring issue in our history. There are some who say Lincoln won the Republican nomination through fraud. Others claim that John F. Kennedy won the presidential election by voter fraud in Chicago. More recently, many claims of fraud have been made in the 2020 election.

Let's be honest. Voter and election fraud do exist. People have been arrested, tried, and jailed for committing voter fraud. To what extent election fraud exists is hotly debated. Most people would agree that any voter fraud is too much voter fraud.

There have been three amendments to the US Constitution related to suffrage or the right to vote.No other issue has been addressed as an amendment more often. It is clearly an issue of paramount importance. The result today is that any citizen of the United States over the age of 18 has the right to vote, regardless of race, creed, color, religion, sex, sexual preference, or gender identity.

At the federal and constitutional level, there are only two

requirements to vote. You must be a citizen and at least 18 years old. At the state and local levels, there are registration and residency requirements. Most states require some form of identification to verify that a potential voter meets these four requirements. The Democrats are trying to federalize almost all election laws through House Resolution 1 and Senate Resolution 1. Simultaneously, Republicans are passing state laws they feel will secure the election process.

Democrat lawmakers want to remove all identification requirements while Republicans want photo ID at the polls. The fight over cleaning voter registration rolls falls along similar lines. In many states, Democrats fight against cleaning voter rolls and use divisive language to make it appear sinister. Efforts to clear voter rolls are called a purge and somehow considered racist.

Voter rolls are notoriously bloated. People are more mobile than ever. When we move even a few blocks, we have to update our voter registration. Often the old one doesn't go away, and a new registration is made. People move across state lines. People die and remain on the voter rolls for years. A case recently before the Pennsylvania Supreme Court requires that a voter suspected of being deceased has to be verified against the Social Security death database before removal is allowed.

Most experts agree that mail-in voting is the most difficult to police. Signature matching is not 100% and is really the only security measure that can be used for ballots through the mail. Couple the inherent lack of security with mail-in ballots and bloated voter rolls, and it becomes easy to see the potential for fraud. With the tremendous expansion of the use of vote by mail during the Coronavirus pandemic, more election security issues have been raised.

The potential for election fraud could be drastically reduced by one simple idea. Allow voter registration to expire. If voter registration were to expire annually, then anyone who moves or dies is automatically removed from the rolls when they don't renew the registration. Send an annual renewal notice. Make the renewal process as simple as possible but require renewal.

The fight over racist purges would be replaced by an automated process that applies to everyone. The removal of unauthorized voters from the rolls also removes a point of potential election fraud and drastically reduces even the appearance of impropriety.

* * *

# 16

# One Bill, One Topic

Politics in the United States has become far too complex. Simple single issues are almost never even addressed by our elected lawmakers. Single-issue bills become Christmas tree bills. Every lawmaker with a cause attaches an amendment like an ornament. Money and lobbyists become involved with every proposal. Simple bills become thousands of pages long overnight. In short, Washington D.C. just doesn't understand "simple" anymore.

Our founding fathers wrote the framework of a brand new form of government in 4,543 words. The United States Constitution defined the three branches of government and enumerated the powers of each branch in less than 5,000 words. Include the 27 amendments and today's constitution is still only 7,591 words. Today our federal government regularly passes laws containing over 8,000 pages. The Constitution can be read and understood by anyone with a tenth-grade reading level. Nothing our government does in the twenty-first century can be understood without a juris doctorate degree, if then.

It is time We The People return simplicity to Washington

D.C. It is time our elected officials start writing laws that everyone can understand. Citizens of the United States should not have to hire professionals just to pay taxes. Entrepreneurs should not have to hire attorneys just to decipher the mountain of regulations from multiple agencies when trying to start a business. It is time the government starts doing its job for the people and stops governing over the people. We have a right to understand the laws our government passes.

HR 46: One Bill, One Subject Transparency Act would be a big step towards understanding federal law again. HR 46 would do more for getting Washington, DC under control than any other bill presented in decades. One Bill, One Subject would eliminate huge amounts of shady deals and earmarks while providing transparency We The People so desperately need. The official summary of the bill states:

(a) One Subject.—Each bill or joint resolution shall embrace no more than one subject.

(b) Subject In Title.—The subject of a bill or joint resolution shall be clearly and descriptively expressed in the title.

(c) Appropriation Bills.—An appropriations bill shall not contain any general legislation or change of existing law provision which is not germane to the subject matter of the underlying bill. This subsection does not prohibit any provision imposing limitations upon the expenditure of appropriated funds.

Passing HR 46 One Bill, One Subject Transparency Act could be the greatest administrative accomplishment of the United

States since passing the Bill of Rights in 1791.

* * *

# Epilogue

We originally had a government of the people, for the people, and by the people, yet we have created a ruling political class and a bureaucratic state to lord over us and spend our money with reckless abandon. Our foundation established a simple government with simple rules that anyone could understand.

Technology has advanced far beyond anything our founding fathers could have imagined. Society, embracing that technology, has progressed as well. Most of the founders would be proud of the civil rights protections we have adopted. Yet, they would be appalled by the national debt, the welfare state, the recent turn to an equity focus, and other areas of "progress."

A large part of the beauty of the United States Constitution is its simplicity. Our political class largely avoids simple ideas. It is time We The People elect representatives who will work to return simplicity to our bureaucratic overlords. One or two representatives or a president with this focus is not sufficient. We must instill the virtue of simplicity in the vast majority of officials at all levels of government. Liberal or conservative, Democrat or Republican, elected representatives that write bills that can be understood without hiring an attorney.

# Afterword

Your Majesty, the Honorable King George III,

I have spent my life in service to the crown. When assigned to my current post in the American Colonies I was not pleased, but I am here to serve Your Majesty. For years now I have reported upon the government of your colonies to the best of my ability. Never have I dared to suggest a course of action. Please forgive my boldness today, My Lord.

I write to you this day with a report from the Americas and a humble request that if granted will return glory to the British Empire, in time.

The rebellious colonies of the Americas have added to their new Constitution. They are calling these amendments the Bill of Rights.  The colonists claim that their rights come from the almighty creator and not from their government. These simpletons allow dirty peasants to have the same rights as the noble class.

Their greatest folly may be in that the government they have designed is slow-moving. The head of government, what they are calling a president, has very little power. All of their leaders are replaced every few years, most by public election. In time, these flaws shall certainly make their experiment in government ineffectual.

If I may be so bold as to counsel Your Majesty, have patience, my Lord. The government these rebels have designed is destined to fail. The arrogance to think they don't need the consistent power of a king be evidence. These new states will destroy themselves with their own liberty. The uneducated rabble will not vote wisely. The moment that the unwashed masses realize they elect those who control the purse strings the republic will be crushed by its own spending. It shall not be long until your colonies will beg for your good grace and protection again. I say again, patience, your majesty, patience.

A loyal and humble servant

28 December 1791

# About the Author

**PETER SEREFINE** is a high school educated proud US Navy veteran.  In 2018, the political turmoil in the United States compelled Peter to take a stand.  His first book, "Progress, Really?", was written to inspire others to question the direction of social and political progress.  Peter went on to Host the Liberty Lighthouse on Mojo 5-0 Radio where his fellow hosts have dubbed him as having the best beard in radio.  After two failed marriages, Peter now lives in a small Victorian Pennsylvania town with his soulmate, Staisha Hancock.

**You can connect with me on:**
- https://www.liberty-lighthouse.com
- https://twitter.com/PSerefine
- https://www.facebook.com/PSerefine

# Also by Peter Serefine

## Progress, Really?

The first thing Peter ever wrote to be published is a condensed review of social progress in the United States of America. The author makes observations of controversial topics and hopes to inspire the reader to ask some very important questions. Where is social progress taking our country? Has the march of progress become a sprint? Is America approaching a second revolution?

## A More Tyrannical King

"A More Tyrannical King" is a thought-provoking exploration of the shifting dynamics of government power and its implications for the preservation of our cherished principles of freedom, liberty, and limited government. From the perspective of constitutional originalism, this book presents a compelling case that the current federal government has become more oppressive than the despotic rule of King George III during the American Revolution.

9 798201 526825